Praise for *Grandparenting Screen Kids*

If you're a grandparent, you need this book! Gary Chapman and Arlene Pellicane have done a masterful job of offering practical activities and hands-on projects that will fully engage your screen-hungry grandchildren. *Grandparenting Screen Kids* is a must-read for anyone who wants to make a positive and lasting difference in the lives of the next generation.

CAROL KENT | Speaker and author of *Staying Power: Building a Stronger Marriage When Life Sends Its Worst*

I loved this book! My wife and I tried to create a media-safe home when our kids were growing up but now the challenges are even more complicated with our grandchildren. Gary Chapman, whom I admire as much as anyone I know, and Arlene Pellicane, a wonderful mom and writer, have combined to give us a practical, purposeful plan to be legacy-giving grandparents with solid ideas on screen time with our grandkids. You will benefit greatly from this book.

JIM BURNS | President, HomeWord; author of *Doing Life with Your Adult Children: Keep Your Mouth Shut and the Welcome Mat Out*

Deep down, what do kids want more than screen time? They crave time with grandparents who spoil them, laugh with them, share memories, bake, build, explore, and sometimes even play video games and watch YouTube! Gary Chapman and Arlene Pellicane take an issue of grave concern and turn it into a blessing!

JAY PAYLEITNER | National speaker and bestselling author of *52 Things Kids Need from a Dad* and *What If God Wrote Your Bucket List?*

What a needed book! With world events turning us all more and more to our screens, we desperately need guidance on how to best handle screen time instead of screen time handling us! We love that Dr. Gary Chapman and Arlene Pellicane have built a two-way bridge between generations with *Grandparenting Screen Kids*. We are grandparents to children aged infant to thirteen years old, and this practical, biblical, and helpful book is a godsend to all relationships.

PAM AND BILL FARREL | Authors of fifty-plus books, including the bestselling *Men Are Like Waffles, Women Are Like Spaghetti*

Grandparenting in this digital age can be tricky, especially if you are a slow adapter like me! This book will help you get smart about tech so you can learn to have fun in their world and enjoy grandparenting once again.

KEN DAVIS | Inspirational speaker and bestselling author

One of the common questions I'm regularly asked by grandparents is, "Do you have a resource to help me navigate technology and screens with my grandchildren?" Well, now we do! In this book, Gary and Arlene offer valuable guidance and helpful ideas that every grandparent will benefit from. This book will help you avoid media pitfalls, utilize screens intentionally, and develop deep relationships with your grandchildren! I can't wait to see the fruit that comes from grandparents putting these ideas into practice.

JOSH MULVIHILL | Author, *Biblical Grandparenting* and *Discipling Your Grandchildren*, GospelShapedFamily.com

When our young grandsons come over, they all want to use my iPad! My wife and I experience the issue addressed in *Grandparenting Screen Kids* nearly every time they are at our house. I have found this book is wonderfully helpful—great principles, solid advice, and a careful distinction between the responsibilities of parents and grandparents. Gary Chapman and Arlene Pellicane have teamed up to provide great guidance for this dilemma that nearly every family faces. I heartily recommend this book; in today's world, it is a "must-add" to your library of grandparenting helps.

LARRY FOWLER | Founder, The Legacy Coalition

When it comes to the relationship I have with my grandkids, my #1 desire is to make every moment a significant one that will turn their hearts toward Jesus. Devices oftentimes can get in the way and derail great intentions. This book has reignited my resolve to claim every moment. It's given me a host of approaches to take in order to set aside devices that distract, but it's also provided me with replacement strategies. This is a fantastic must-read for grandparents.

TINA HOUSER | Writer, speaker, editor, and children's pastor

What's a grandparent to do when we differ with our grandkids on screen habits? I'm grateful that while distanced, we are able to communicate on FaceTime or Skype with loved ones. But there may be occasional tech tension when the younger generation (who have *always* known smartphones and computers) visit us. That's why I highly recommend Arlene Pellicane and Gary Chapman's new book *Grandparenting Screen Kids*. Finally, we have some very practical suggestions both for monitoring healthy usage and offering alternative activities. Emphasizing basic manners was a plus, as were the reminders that our kids are the parents and we need to support their rules. Family relationships are a delicate dance, but resources like this can truly help all generations learn to interact in community.

LUCINDA SECREST MCDOWELL | Author of *Soul Strong* and *Life-Giving Choices*

GRANDPARENTING
Screen Kids

HOW TO HELP, WHAT TO SAY, AND WHERE TO BEGIN

GARY CHAPMAN
AND ARLENE PELLICANE

NORTHFIELD PUBLISHING
CHICAGO

Scriptures taken from the Holy Bible, New International Version®, NIV®. Copyright © 1973, 1978, 1984, 2011 by Biblica, Inc.™ Used by permission of Zondervan. All rights reserved worldwide. www.zondervan.com. The "NIV" and "New International Version" are trademarks registered in the United States Patent and Trademark Office by Biblica, Inc.™

Some names have been changed to protect the privacy of individuals.

Edited by Elizabeth Cody Newenhuyse
Interior and cover design: Erik M. Peterson
Cover illustration of cardboard phone copyright © 2019 by Marie Maerz/Adobe Stock (105871809).
Cover illustrations of people copyright © 2018 by Sudowoodo /iStock (1057675582).
Cover illustration of speech bubbles copyright © 2019 by Marie Maerz/Shutterstock (392934271).
All rights reserved for the above illustrations.
Chapman author photo: P.S.Photography
Pellicane author photo: Anthony Amorteguy

Library of Congress Cataloging-in-Publication Data

Names: Chapman, Gary D., 1938- author. | Pellicane, Arlene, 1971- author.
Title: Grandparenting screen kids : how to help, what to say, and where to
  begin / Gary Chapman and Arlene Pellicane.
Description: Chicago, IL : Northfield Publishing, [2020] | Includes
  bibliographical references. | Summary: "Grandparenting in the Digital
  Age Things aren't what they once were. As younger generations become
  increasingly immersed in the endless presence of tech, older generations
  struggle finding common ground to relate.The gap between grandparent and
  grandchild may feel wider than ever. Grandparenting Screen Kids is a
  grandparent's guide to start bridging this gap. Relationship expert Gary
  Chapman along with coauthor Arlene Pellicane will help you understand
  this different (and often troubling) world of iPads, YouTube and video
  games. They will offer activities to keep your grandkids occupied
  without screens and assist you in navigating differences with your adult
  children. It's easy to feel overwhelmed, under informed, and physically
  unable to meet the demands of active grandkids. That's why this
  companion guide to the book Screen Kids has been written to connect you
  to information and encouragement. Technology isn't going anywhere and
  your grandkids need you more than ever to teach them what computers
  can't"-- Provided by publisher.
Identifiers: LCCN 2020017849 (print) | LCCN 2020017850 (ebook) | ISBN
  9780802420701 (paperback) | ISBN 9780802499028 (ebook)
Subjects: LCSH: Grandparenting. | Grandparents. | Internet and children.
Classification: LCC HQ759.9 .C42 2020 (print) | LCC HQ759.9 (ebook) | DDC
  306.874/5--dc23
LC record available at https://lccn.loc.gov/2020017849
LC ebook record available at https://lccn.loc.gov/2020017850

We hope you enjoy this book from Northfield Publishing. Our goal is to provide high-quality, thought-provoking books and products that connect truth to your real needs and challenges. For more information on other books and products that will help you with all your important relationships, go to northfieldpublishing.com or write to:

Northfield Publishing
820 N. LaSalle Boulevard
Chicago, IL 60610

1 3 5 7 9 10 8 6 4 2

Printed in the United States of America

CONTENTS

Introduction: We're Not in Kansas Anymore

Do you remember watching *The Wizard of Oz* on television with your family? Airing this classic was an annual tradition on American network television from 1959 to 1991. How and what we watch on television has changed a lot since then. As Dorothy famously said, "We're not in Kansas anymore."

We no longer gather on the couch regularly as a family to watch television. I (Gary) have pleasant memories of watching Christmas classics when our grandchildren were younger. They lived in another state but always came for Christmas. These shared experiences stimulated conversation and built memories. I (Arlene) remember many evenings watching shows like *Wheel of Fortune, Jeopardy!,* and *Matlock* with my grandma.

Today, grandkids have their own phones or tablets. They are watching programs and playing video games *alone*. Screen time is largely a solo sport. Grandparents can watch what they want on the big screen while their grandchildren watch a cartoon on a laptop or iPad. Some would call this progress, but many grandparents don't find the changes satisfying or joyous. Instead of having a unifying effect, separate screens under one roof can have a distancing, even polarizing effect.

But does tech have to divide us? No. Technology can bridge gaps instead of create them. Take video chatting, for example. According to an AARP survey, "38 percent of American grandparents . . . sometimes or often use video chat to communicate with their grandkids."[1] It's pretty amazing that a grandfather who lives in Hawaii could watch a grandchild play the piano in Michigan, and applaud in real time through FaceTime. A digitally savvy grandma might follow her granddaughter on social media to learn about her friends and interests in order to have more meaningful conversations. Grandparents can regularly video chat with their faraway grands so that when they do visit for Christmas, they already know one another. No need to warm up to each other; the relationship has already been primed by technology. It seems like technology can be a huge blessing when you're geographically apart—but a curse when you're sitting in the same room together.

What to do?

If you're a grandparent who spends any amount of time with your grandchildren, you're very aware of the challenges. And we're here to help.

Grandparenting Screen Kids can be read as a stand-alone book or as a companion to our book *Screen Kids: 5 Relational Skills Every Child Needs in a Tech-Driven World*. If you are the primary caregiver for your grandchild, we believe reading both *Grandparenting Screen Kids* and *Screen Kids* will be very beneficial and illuminating.

In the following chapters, you're going to learn how to help, what to say, and where to begin. Your grandchild needs lots of love. As a grandparent, you are uniquely created to speak life to your grandson or granddaughter through your words of affirmation, physical touch, gifts, time, and acts of service. No video game can provide this kind of love. No social media app comes close. Don't allow popular culture or the bad behavior of your grandkids to deter you. The wisdom of grandparents is never outdated, and it's never more needed.

The Superhero of the Toy Kingdom

What can I do when my grandchild just wants to use their tablet all day?

Where do we start? Kids have so many digital distractions these days—as we're sure you've noticed. There is something powerful competing with you for your grandchild's attention. It's not a brownie straight from the oven or a basketball waiting to be bounced. It's an iPad, or other brand of tablet. And it's the superhero of the toy kingdom. That slim rectangle is the gateway to so many adventures. It makes other activities look lame in comparison.

Perhaps you remember a time your grandchildren

came to visit before screens took over. You read books and colored. You made popcorn and then watched a movie together. Visits look different now. Your grandchild wants one thing more than anything else: time to play on the iPad.

What makes the iPad so alluring, anyway? The tablet has been painstakingly designed to engage your grandson or granddaughter with an endless adrenaline drip of excitement and entertainment. Our brains are drawn to intermittent, unexpected rewards—and that's exactly what this device constantly provides. Remember that excited feeling of going to the mailbox because there might be a letter for you inside? That's what it is like when your grandchild starts using the iPad. Surprises await, and the brain craves that hit of dopamine, the hormone associated with pleasure.

Did you have a favorite television show when you were a child? You had to wait for a certain time each week to watch. There were commercials, and way back you couldn't mute or fast-forward through them. You couldn't tape it. The show ended after thirty or sixty minutes. Maybe you didn't like the next show, so it was easy to turn off the TV and go do something else. The iPad doesn't provide stopping points like this, but offers a continuous stream of new and exciting things to watch, almost commercial-free. *You* have to create the interruptions, or else your grandkids will just keep watching.

NANA'S HOUSE IS DIFFERENT

Maybe you've seen the following slogans on decorative signs with Nana's house rules:

Grandkids welcome
Parents by appointment
Endless hugs and kisses
Laugh—Giggle—Snuggle
Kitchen open twenty-four hours
Eat cookies, tell stories

You've probably never seen slogans like "Unlimited video games" or "Stare at your device for hours" on a sign. That's not the connection and fun associated with going to Nana and Papa's house. You can craft your own house rules whether your grandchild visits occasionally or all day every Monday, Wednesday, and Friday. Make your home distinctive, reflecting the values that are important to you. You don't have to cater to your grandkids' pleas for video games or more tablet time. Your house can provide a totally different experience from the norm. That difference is both doable and desirable.

If you are having a hard time wrangling the iPad away from your toddler or teenager, try one of these solutions:

iPad Zones—Have particular zones in the home where the iPad is allowed and other zones where it is off limits. Some tablet-free zones that come to mind are around the dinner table, the kitchen, the backyard, bedrooms, and bathrooms.

iPad Hours—You can post operating hours on a piece of paper such as "iPads allowed between 11 a.m. and noon."

iPad Naptime—With younger kids, you can tell them that their tablet needs a nap. You can fold a cloth napkin to create a little bed. Cover up the iPad, read it a story, and let it lie dormant for a few hours.

iPad Check—Copy the coat check service at the

theatre. Upon entering your home, your grandchild can check in his or her device. You can place it in your closet for safekeeping and even issue a little ticket to claim it later (which would be fun for younger kids).

Before you begin a new routine for iPad use during visits, have a chat with your grandchildren about the new rules, preferably over some ice cream. Your grandkids may not embrace these new rules. In fact, they will probably throw a fit at some point! Stand firm, however, with your boundaries, and before long, they will become the new normal at Nana and Papa's house.

You may need to begin a new routine for *your* screen use as well.

By the way, you may need to begin a new routine for *your* screen use as well. If you are asking your grandchildren to trade their video games for books, but you are constantly answering text messages and scrolling through news sites, that will not go unnoticed.

BUT WHAT CAN WE DO INSTEAD?

Creative bloggers have written about "money-free" weekends, coming up with lists of free family activities. How about a "tablet-free" weekend (or weekdays) for you to enjoy more quality moments with your grandchildren? You know about activities like drawing, coloring, board games, reading stories, dancing, singing, playing dress-up, and blowing bubbles. Here are some additional ideas to replace iPad time with something much richer:

Go on a nature walk. Before you head out, make a list of things to find like a green leaf, a rock bigger than a shoebox, a robin, etc. Let your grandchildren know that walking is really good for your health as a grandparent, so the more nature walks you take together, the better.

Visit the library. The library is a forgotten treasure. Check out books regularly and keep them at your house. Pick books for yourself so your grandchild sees your interest in reading as well. Once your grandchild has a favorite author, you can search for that author in the library's catalog and reserve those books for future visits. If your grandchild has a special interest like science or travel, he or she can explore those too. It's a great feeling to walk up to the "hold" shelf and see a desired book waiting there for you.

Chalk drawing contest. Have the grandkids head outside to the sidewalk and have a chalk drawing contest. The parents can decide on the winner or, to add a community twist, you can ask your neighbor to act as the judge.

Visit a fire station. Many fire stations welcome visitors. Call before stopping by and inquire about a short tour. Who knows? They may let your grandchild spray the fire hose or climb into the fire truck.

Hide-and-seek. Hide-and-seek is more humorous when grandparents participate! You may have to adapt the pace and hiding places (you may not be able to crawl under the desk anymore). But no doubt your grandkids will have more fun if you play too.

Family album day. Take out your old photo albums to show your grandkids your siblings and family members. Share some funny memories about your childhood. Write a few letters or draw some pictures together for the family members pictured. What a treat it would be for an aunt or uncle to receive a drawing or letter from your grandchild!

Lego building contest. This can take place over a few visits if the kids want to build something elaborate. They can also team up to build a Lego scene together to reveal to their parents. The Lego creation can be kept under a sheet until it's complete. Unveil it with great pomp and circumstance.

Bake something together. What beats the fragrance of cookies or cupcakes baking in the oven? Not much! Have your grandkids help with measuring out the flour, mixing the ingredients, scooping out the dough, even frosting. ("Scraping the bowl" allowed!)

Build an ice castle. Fill up a bunch of ice cube trays and Popsicle trays the night before your grandkids visit. Or better yet, they can fill the trays if they see you more than once a week. When the ice cubes are ready, pop out the ice and build an ice castle outside. If it's hot, the castle will melt quickly but it will feel so nice and cool on the skin. If it's wintertime, that ice castle might last for days.

NO TABLET CAN TEACH LIFE SKILLS

Jerry is a father and grandfather who did some everyday errands in an unusually clever way. He would purposefully take his grandchildren to the grocery store not to shop but to learn *how* to shop. "Here's how you pick a good apple," he would say to his eight-year-old grandson. "This is a cheap price for chicken," he would point out to his ten-year-old granddaughter. He wanted his grandkids to know how to shop for themselves when they were older.

Jerry would do the same thing at the bank, explaining how to use the ATM machine, demonstrating a transaction with the bank teller, and showing them how to write a check. Perhaps more than ever, kids need practical training on these kinds of life skills. If you have a teen grandchild, you may be the best person to help that girl or boy learn how to drive. You may have the time and you definitely have the experience. Hours behind the wheel together will become a sacred space for conversation—and perhaps prayer!

Your teen grandchild may appear to be much more interested in using an iPad or phone, but you have so much more to offer. You can:

Teach your grandchild how to prepare five meals. Most young people know how to order food on their phones, but they don't know anything about cooking themselves. You can gift them with the ability to prepare five meals. When they make those meals in a tiny apartment far from home for the first time, they will be thinking of you.

Run through a mock job interview. Have your grandchild dress up for the interview and you can give feedback on their appearance. Pretend to be the person responsible for the hiring, ask relevant questions, and then give your suggestions. Insist on eye contact and keep practicing the conversation until he or she is comfortable and confident.

Practice phone skills. Many kids lean into texting and emailing, but they are mortified to make a voice call. They even avoid ordering pizza over the phone. Practice talking on the phone during their visits. Let them know it's for the purpose of getting comfortable with talking on the phone, not because you want the phone out all the time.

Ask your grandchild to be your personal trainer. My (Arlene's) parents, who are in their seventies, need to exercise more, but they don't enjoy going to the gym. So my kids go over to their house and exercise with them from time to time. "Come on, Nana," Ethan will say, "give me twenty-five more leg raises and then we'll take a break." Your grandkids can help you get healthier and learn the skill of coaching in the process.

The presence of tablets may be new and pervasive, but never underestimate your presence as a grandparent. Your love is more powerful than pixels and cute cat videos. Don't give up on establishing and enforcing restrictions with your grandchild's iPad. The more they have your undivided attention, the less they will crave the electronic thrills of the iPad.

Parental Controls

Working with your adult children, you can use parental controls to set content and privacy restrictions on the iPad or other tablet.

• Go to Settings and tap Screen Time.

- Tap Content & Privacy Restrictions.
- From here, you can limit:
  - Music (clean or explicit)
  - Movies and TV shows (based on ratings)
  - Apps (based on age)
  - Web content (limit adult websites)
  - Multiplayer games (allow or don't allow)

Video Game Wars

*What if I don't agree with the type
of games or the time spent gaming
by my grandkids?*

I (Arlene) was at the grocery store when I over-heard two men chatting together near the onions.

"Has your wife joined you in retirement yet?" one man asked.

"Nope, she's decided that working full-time is much easier than watching the grandkids!"

Can you relate? Running after a preschooler and toddler can be overwhelming . . . to say the least. Video games can seem like a welcome addition. They help keep your grandkids busy and safe. The little ones aren't bumping their heads on tables or putting strange objects into their mouths. But you have second thoughts about how much your little ones like playing games.

Or maybe you have an older grandchild and you're concerned about the violent video games he plays. He says all his friends play games like *Call of Duty* and *Fortnite*. We've come a long way from playing *Asteroids* and *Pac-Man* with quarters in the arcade. Video games are much more mobile, immersive, addictive, and violent than they used to be. When your grandchild asks with a "please" to play a video game, it can be hard to resist. It may even feel futile! But before you hand over your phone, tablet, or gaming device, there are a few things you need to know about video games.

BOYS AND GIRLS PLAY DIFFERENTLY

We tend to think of boys playing video games, not girls. But as girls grow up, many of them will turn into women who play. Sixty-five percent of American adults play video games. The average female video game player is thirty-four, and the average male video game player is thirty-two. Surprisingly, 46 percent of US gamers are women.[1]

Females tend to play very different kinds of games than males. Girls play social and casual games. They are more inclined to play on the go in short spurts on a mobile device or iPad. Males in general like to focus on a smaller number of tasks and dedicate more time to those tasks (think of a boy investing hours into a video game), whereas women tend to have many more tasks, spending shorter amounts of time on each one.

Boys are extremely attracted to video games because they are highly visual, achievement-oriented, and community-based. The animation is so real; your grandson feels as if he is in that battle, surrounded by enemies from a different world. He may not be successful in school, but he can achieve a sense of mastery through gaming. Many games include other players, which taps into your grandson's deep desire to have strong social connections.

THE BIG RISK

Games are designed to deliver small doses of positive feedback to entice players right from the start. Dopamine lights up the pleasure center of the brain. Every time you do something, you get credit. Rewards are tested and delivered at precisely the right intervals, so your grandkids will keep on coming back for more.

Psychologist Kimberly Young coined the phrase "internet addiction" way back in 1995.[2] She says the biggest changes were the introduction of the iPhone and iPad because games became mobile, available to anyone with a device all the time. In addition to treating a string of teenage boys at her Center for Internet Addiction, she began treating females of all ages and personality types.

And, of course, the excessive use of video games is a problem all around the world. Professor Tao Ran is a psychiatrist and treatment center director in China. He believes internet addiction is the number one public threat to the teenage population. He says:

> *We notice that these children have a bias towards virtual reality. They think the real world isn't as*

good as the virtual world. Our research shows that addicts spend more than six hours a day online, not for the purpose of work or studying . . . some kids are so hooked on these games that they think going to the bathroom will affect their performance. So they wear a diaper.[3]

Talk about regression—back to diapers! If you see your grandchild is becoming more and more adamant about playing video games and/or becoming defiant when you direct him or her to another activity, that is a red flag. On the other hand, if your grandchild becomes bored after playing a video game and transitions independently to another activity, that is a good sign that he or she is a casual player.

If you decide to allow gaming, you must watch the specific game first and give it a thumbs-up or a thumbs-down.

GRANDMA AND GRANDPA'S GUIDELINES

It is important for you to decide on guidelines at your house. You can create a new normal from this day forward for your grandchild. You may decide to have a video game-free household (that's what Arlene's parents did). Make it fun and be dramatic about your label of "Grandpa approved!" or "Rejected!" You can explain, "I'm your grandparent and I don't want you to play games that I think will be harmful for you."

Inquire about the rating of the video games your grandchild wants to play before allowing games in your home. We recommend rejecting "Mature" and "Adults Only" games at your house, no matter how old your grandchild is. Here is the ratings guide, according to the Entertainment Software Rating Board:[4]

E—Everyone
May contain minimal cartoon, fantasy or mild violence and/or infrequent use of mild language.

E 10+—Everyone 10+
May contain more cartoon, fantasy or mild violence, mild language and/or minimal suggestive themes.

T—Teen

May contain violence, suggestive themes, crude humor, minimal blood, simulated gambling and/or infrequent use of strong language.

M—Mature 17+

May contain intense violence, blood and gore, sexual content and/or strong language.

AO—Adults Only 18+

May include prolonged scenes of intense violence, graphic sexual content and/or gambling with real currency.

Set time and content limits. Plan to have screens be part of the schedule but not *all* the schedule. Have a reading time, play time, and nap or just quiet time (that's the best part!). Kids thrive on structure and will flourish when you call the shots about how the time will be spent at your house instead of the other way around. Don't let your grandchildren tell you what *they* want to do at *your* home. If you allow them to set the agenda (video games all day long!), they will become almost intolerable guests when they are teenagers.

There are too many stories of young men who enter college only to quit because of a gaming addiction. You can help your grandchild avoid that dead-end future by using the time spent in your home to stoke his interest in the real world.

Papa Says

Check your devices at the door
Kitchen open twenty-four hours (see Nana)
Thirty minutes of TV
No violent video games allowed
Library is always open
Play board games
Let's fix stuff

3

The Lure of YouTube

Is YouTube dangerous for kids?

Years ago, your own kid might have loved watching videos and DVDs, but now it's all about YouTube. YouTube seems like a great place to get free content for kids, but there are dangers most grandparents don't realize. YouTube Kids was created to give your grandchildren a more contained environment, but using YouTube Kids doesn't ensure that only "safe" videos will be delivered.

For example, BBC News reported on a (fake) video of Peppa Pig, star of her own animated series, which looked ordinary at the beginning. But the plot grew darker as a dentist with a huge syringe appeared. Parent and journalist Laura June almost immediately noticed something wasn't right as her three-year-old was watching it. "Peppa does a lot of screaming and crying and the dentist is just a bit sadistic and it's just way, way off what a three-year-old should watch." The animation was crude but the pirated version was close enough that her daughter really thought it was Peppa the Pig. (In the real episode, Peppa is appropriately reassured by a kindly dentist.)[1]

Unfortunately, this is not an isolated case. Hundreds of similar videos of children's cartoon characters, from Mickey Mouse to the princesses of *Frozen*, contained inappropriate themes. The anonymous hacker creators want to reap ad revenue. The innocent consumers and victims are your grandchildren.

WARNING: INAPPROPRIATE VIDEOS AHEAD

The YouTube Kids landing page says, "We work hard to keep videos on YouTube Kids family-friendly and use a mix of automated filters built by our engineering teams, human review, and feedback from parents. . . .

But not all videos have been manually reviewed. If you find something inappropriate that we missed, you can flag it for fast review."[2] The problem is your grandchild can watch a harmful video without your knowledge, and it's unreasonable to think he or she will be flagging it for fast review. It's good to use YouTube Kids instead of the normal YouTube, but you must realize it's not foolproof. With more than five hundred hours of video uploaded to YouTube every minute, it's impossible for each video to land in the appropriate category.[3]

Doctors and mental health experts warn that YouTube is a growing source of anxiety and inappropriate sexual behavior among kids under thirteen. Child psychotherapist Dr. Natasha Daniels reports that YouTube is an ongoing topic of conversation in her practice. Over the last five years, she has seen a rise in cases of children suffering anxiety triggered by YouTube videos. Dr. Daniels says, "There have been times when a child is brought to my office between [the ages of] eight and 10 and they're found doing sexual things: oral sex, kissing and getting naked and acting out sexual poses. This usually indicates some sort of sexual abuse. . . . However, in the last five years, when I follow the trail all the way back, it's YouTube and that's where it ends."[4]

As a grandparent, you can make sure your grandkids are not harmed by looking at inappropriate YouTube videos on your watch. This takes a commitment to be actively involved with what the kids are viewing. When you see your grandkids watching a YouTube video, it's often your signal to run in the opposite direction and get a few things done. But before you head into the other room, join your grandchildren for a few minutes to see what they are watching.

Once you find that grandparent-approved YouTube video channel, subscribe to it so your grandkids don't have to hunt around YouTube looking for something to watch. You can choose subscriptions together with your grandchildren. It takes more time up front, but later it will save you time as you're deciding with your grandchild what is okay to watch. Talking about videos is also a good way to bond with your grandchild by discovering what he or she finds interesting. You can visit CommonSenseMedia.org for tips on making YouTube safer as well as finding movie and TV show reviews.

For younger kids:
We recommend watching . . .

Mister Rogers' Neighborhood
(You can watch free full-length episodes at MisterRogers.org.)

Daniel Tiger's Neighborhood
(You can watch free full-length episodes at PBSKids.org.)

Minno (GoMinno.com)
Curated video subscription plan with the largest online selection of classic *Veggie Tales* and shows like *What's in the Bible* and *Superbook*.

WATCH SMARTER

Unlike grandparents of the (recent) past who had many program choices through cable, today's grandparent has even more options through streaming services like Disney+, Netflix, and YouTube. You may have noticed that once you start streaming content it can be very difficult to stop. This is true of adults (that's why we talk about "bingeing") and it's especially true of children. It starts with just one video, but then another video cues up that looks so interesting. You click to watch, and this cycle just continues, turning minutes into hours. If you see your grandchild is spending way too much time watching YouTube videos, you will need to step in and redirect them to another activity. Very few children will be able to muster the self-discipline to do this independently. You can set a timer for an allotted time such as thirty minutes, and collect the tablet when the timer beeps. You can also use this system for streaming services such as Netflix or Disney+. Set a timer or limit of "two programs" and stick with it.

The huge problem with YouTube and streaming services is they are bottomless.

If you have a DVD or Blu-ray player, use these

wonderful archaic devices instead of YouTube or streaming services. The beauty of putting in a disc is that the show will have a beginning and an ending. Unlike YouTube or streaming services, there is a natural stopping point. The huge problem with YouTube and streaming services is they are bottomless. There are hundreds of choices for kids to pick from. YouTube cues up the next video for your grandchild and starts playing it immediately without your permission! This is not progress toward the development of healthy kids. The older technology of a DVD player is light-years ahead.

What can you do if your grandchild is used to watching one hour or more of YouTube at your house? You might want to invent a new game such as the "YouTube Top Three!" This would entail your grandchild choosing three videos on YouTube for the duration of his or her visit—and that's it. Tell your grandchild to choose wisely, since he or she will only get to pick three. If there is a limit, he or she will be more selective. After this video countdown, begin another activity—going outside, doing a puzzle, helping with a chore, playing with the dog.

Let's face it, the appeal of YouTube is not only strong for kids, it's strong for adults because it keeps our kids safely occupied inside and out of trouble. (And maybe allows us to take a little break.) But these videos aren't always "safe." We can tell ourselves that YouTube is educational, but if we are honest, our grandkids aren't usually learning a second language or practicing math skills on YouTube. Even videos that promote letter recognition and reading are a poor substitute for children listening to and talking with you.

Make your home a place where YouTube is used sparingly. Instead of your grandkids' watching YouTube child celebrities play with cars or dress up in costumes, make your grandkids play for themselves in real life.

4

Clash of the Caregivers

What if I don't agree with the screen time rules of my adult children?

Claire's three grandchildren watch hours of YouTube and Netflix at home. She doesn't agree with how lenient her daughter is with screen time, but she doesn't say much about it. "I don't want to alienate my daughter. I don't want to upset her or give her any reason to stop bringing the grandkids to visit." Sound familiar?

Maybe you're concerned by the amount of screen time your grandkids consume or the violent games they are allowed to play. Or maybe you are the one

Remember: Your children are the parents, not you.

who wants to spoil your grandchild with the latest iPhone, and your daughter is pleading with you to reconsider. Many times, grandparents want to tell their adult children what they, the grandparents, think is right. Typically, this conversation doesn't go over very well.

We're not opposed to grandparents bringing up topics and sharing concerns. But, grandparents, remember: Your children are the parents, not you. Parents have the primary responsibility for raising children. Grandparents can help, and that's a very important role of being an advisor, but unsolicited advice is rarely heeded or welcomed.

You might read something in this book or in *Screen Kids* that you want to pass along to your kids because you found it helpful and informative. You can casually pass it along, but don't keep harping on it. Ultimately, you have to back off. If you repeatedly communicate your disapproval, that's going to put an emotional barrier between you and your child. That wedge may jeopardize your access to your grandkids.

What if you are the primary caregiver for your grandchildren? If you spend more time with them than their parents do, you have a great opportunity to impact the lives of your grandkids. Many grandparents don't have this opportunity because they live too far away. Make the most of the time you spend together—have fun, enjoy sharing in their lives, and don't be afraid to impart your values.

COPING WITH RESENTMENT

We want to add some comments here that don't relate only to kids and screens, but to grandparents and caregiving. Many adults dream of their retirement and the freedom of spending their time however they wish. But grandkids can get in the way of this hard-earned independence, strapping grandparents with caregiving, while their adult kids go into the workforce. Be candid with your feelings. If you feel like you are being used, there's a place to honestly talk with your child. You might say something like, "You know, honey, I've been keeping the kids every Tuesday, Wednesday, and Thursday afternoon for you. I'm going to have to change our Thursday schedule because I am going to be joining a group of ladies for a book club. You'll need to find other arrangements for Thursdays."

Bring up the topic in terms of changes that need to be made. Resist the temptation to blurt out, "I'm getting tired of you just coming and dumping your kids on me. I resent it!" That may be how you are feeling, but we don't say everything that we feel. If you are feeling resentful, ask yourself why you would rather not have the grandchildren so often. Is it because there is something else you need to carve out time for that gives you purpose? Is it because they are not well behaved so it's just too draining? If you didn't see the grandchildren at all, would you miss them and want them back? Be honest with yourself and then negotiate with your child to make helpful changes. Avoid lashing out at your child, who may respond with equal fury and hastily declare, "Fine! I won't bring the kids at all!"

"GRANDSHARENTING"

You may wonder what this word means. Grandsharenting is a term to describe when grandparents post pictures of their grandkids on social media, often without the parents' consent. Grandparents used to proudly show off photos kept in plastic sleeves in their wallets. Now the photos are digital and easy to share on social media. But some parents do not want their children online for anyone to see. They're worried about privacy issues and identity theft.

A *Wall Street Journal* article about grandsharenting describes one grandfather who works in the entertainment industry in New York. He texts his daughter for permission to post photos of his toddler grandson. Her answer is usually no. He estimates he has posted no more than four photos of her son. He said, "I respect my daughter's

As you demonstrate respect for your son or daughter's wishes, they will become more open to hearing your opinions and advice.

43

wishes. If she doesn't want me to post my grandson's pictures, I absolutely honor that while periodically I may beg her to allow me to post a cute one."[1]

This bedrock of respect for one another will carry you through many clashes over caregiving. As you demonstrate respect for your son or daughter's wishes, they will become more open to hearing your opinions and advice. It can be "grand" to share in the responsibilities of child training with your adult kids as you value each other's perspective. Look for opportunities to encourage your adult son or daughter with words of affirmation—not disapproval.

But I'm Exhausted!

How can I get my grandkids engaged in non–screen time activities when I don't have the energy to keep up with them?

When your three grandkids are running through the house screaming, you might think, "There's a reason God gives us children when we're younger!" It can be physically exhausting to watch your grandchildren day after day. Screens may seem like the only way to keep your sanity (and take a seat once in a while). How can you get your grandkids to calm down with something other than a screen?

HYPER KIDS AND SCREEN TIME

Are your grandkids literally running around in circles at your house? Pediatrician and researcher Dimitri Christakis created an experiment with mice and television that will shed light on hyperactive behavior. His lab mice had speakers above and lights around them, and were exposed to TV six hours a day for forty-two days. It turned out these overstimulated mice acted very differently than normal mice. In a square space, the normal mice stuck to moving along the walls, sticking to the corners, never venturing to the middle of the room. The overstimulated mice, on the other hand, ran here, there, and everywhere. The travel pathway of the normal mice created a square. The travel pathway of the TV-watching mice looked more like an abstract painting with squiggles going in every direction. The mice in the TV experiment were much more hyperactive and risk taking than the normal mice.

The next test was called "the novel object recognition." When a novel object was placed in the box, the normal mice spent 75 percent of an allotted time examining that object. But the overstimulated mice didn't even care about the novel object and didn't examine it.[1] It's like if you give new toy blocks to a child who doesn't have much screen time, he most likely will play with those blocks for a while. But if you give the novel blocks to a screen-saturated youngster, he might look at them briefly, but then toss them aside for more screen time. If you want your grandchildren to spend some quiet time at your home playing with toys, reading, or coloring, you will want to reduce, not increase, screen time.

Certainly there are explanations other than "too much screen time" for kids who are bouncing off the walls. Too much sugar, fatigue, needing to go outside and let off steam . . . all these things can lead to restless hyperactivity. But the overstimulation that screens pour into young brains is something wise grandparents need to monitor.

HAVE FUN!

When you have time with your grandchildren, it's important to enjoy some playtime—just having fun together. Now . . . it's unreasonable to think you will be playing together the *whole* time. You have other work to do, and you don't have limitless energy. You can explain this to your grandchildren so they can adjust their expectation of having an energetic play buddy all day long. But it is good to establish a pattern of having a certain time dedicated to playing together.

My (Arlene's) parents bought a Ping-Pong table to play with each other and also to play with the grandkids. My parents have gotten so good that my kids, who are in high school and sixth grade, really have to try to beat them! My parents are not very athletic, so if they can do it, pretty much anyone can. They also love to play cards with the kids.

Karolyn and I (Gary) have an air hockey table at home. Our two grandkids lived three hours away and as soon as they were old enough, we started playing air hockey together. Now my grandson, who is a sophomore in college, will visit and say, "Okay, Grandpa, I'm going to beat you this time!" Of course, he always wins, and we continue making wonderful memories playing air hockey together. During visits, we set up the card table and put out board games. Sometimes it is the four of us playing; sometimes it's Karolyn and the kids, or just the grandkids. You want your home to have activities easily accessible to bring the family together. It doesn't have to be costly. A few dollars at the local thrift store will buy you a board game, chess set, badminton racquets, or puzzles. You can find games and activities that the grandchildren can do together without you, giving you some time for rest. When you take screens out of the equation, siblings often rediscover the fun of playing with each other. After all, there's no one else to play with! This bonding time cannot be underestimated. When siblings are on individual screens or watching a program together, they aren't really interacting.

When you take screens out of the equation, siblings often rediscover the fun of playing with each other.

You can go to the library and get stacks of books, setting up your own library in your family room or a corner of your living room. Your grandkids can pretend to check out books from you and then sit with hot cocoa and instrumental music playing in the background while they read. When they are too young to read, you can read to them and then they can draw pictures and color afterward. Make reading time part of every visit. You won't be as tired running after your grandkids, and they will be much more ready for school with hours logged in your library.

The goal is to build memories together with your grandkids. If time and resources allow, take your grandchildren on trips with you. It might be as luxurious as a cruise or as simple as a thirty-minute drive away to rent a lake house or stay at the beach. These happy memories will be in your grandchildren's minds when they become parents and grandparents someday. Our (Gary's) family gets together each year for one week at the beach. Our kids and grandkids have said it's their favorite week of the entire year.

If a week's vacation isn't an option, a special, day-long outing to the zoo, the tallest building in your city, live (and age-appropriate) theatre, or something completely different like visiting a civil-rights museum or touring a working farm will long be remembered by your grandkids. Don't forget, too, individual outings for your grands!

Time for Grandpa's Nap

My (Arlene's) father is a retired family physician. When he would watch the kids when they were young, they would often play doctor. But he was the patient! My daughter Lucy would take out her toy doctor kit to examine her patient. My dad would make up all sorts of ailments to prolong the appointment. Lucy got to have fun playing doctor, and my father got to lie down on the comfortable couch for a very long spell!

TAKING CARE OF YOU

One grandma writes, "I had a wonderful time with my grandsons and really enjoyed being present for Caden's fourth birthday. However, I have a better understanding of God giving little ones to young people. I am a little worn out!"

Too bad there's not a magic formula for staying healthy to keep up with your grandkids, but there are a few basic principles I (Gary) have followed in my own life. Giving attention to what you eat is very important. I eat a lot of fruits and vegetables. You must also stay as active as you can. Walking is what I primarily do. My grandchildren are grown, so I am no longer chasing them, but I spend plenty of time in airports walking quickly to catch my next flight.

I have a little routine of wake-up exercises that I do each morning. Beginning and sustaining healthy habits is something you can do at any age. None of us knows how long we will be healthy. We just do the best we can to take care of our bodies by getting enough sleep, exercise, and proper nutrition. Take time to take care of yourself, because a healthier you will benefit your grandkids now and in the future. Don't let doctor's appointments or medication refills slide. Carve out time for rest and relaxation.

We never know when a disease might affect us. We must adapt and operate with our limitations, whatever those limitations are. You might not be able to do everything you see other grandparents doing, but you can focus on what you can do. When you feel exhausted, a short nap may make all the difference between feeling despondent and hopeful. Work with your kids to set a doable pace of caregiving. You're not just taking care of your grandkids—you've also got to take care of yourself.

6

Making Common Courtesy Common Again

How can I teach my grandchild manners and common courtesy if she won't look up from her device?

Are kids more or less polite than they were twenty years ago? That's probably a pretty easy question to answer. Kids today are ruder than generations past. There is more cursing on the playground, and more foul language in books, videos, and even emblazoned on T-shirts. Kids and teens are often oblivious to those around them because they are engrossed in a screen. They bully one another on social media and leave crude comments. Many boys and girls have never been taught proper manners. Grandparents can play a pivotal role in making common courtesy common again.

When talking to grandparents about common courtesy, we hear comments like:

We taught our grandkids to say hello and greet people when they enter a room. It's a way to show we are grateful for one another.

We mirrored the behavior first, calling adults Miss Susan or Mr. Tim. Manners are never out of style.

We insisted on eye contact when greeting others and smiling.

We instructed our grandkids to put down all tech as a sign of respect when talking with someone.

When your grandkids come to your house, train them to put their devices down and greet you with a hug, smile, and eye contact. Model this behavior over and over to them, even if they are stiff as a board and staring blankly at you. This is practice for greeting adults in the future.

Your home can become etiquette central. This

doesn't mean you have to become an Emily Post expert. It just means you can teach your grandchildren basic manners that will (unfortunately) set them apart from many of their peers.

BASIC MANNERS FOR ALL AGES

Manner #1: Say please and thank you.

Role-play with your grandkids different scenarios when it would be appropriate to say "please" and "thank you." When they ask for something like milk at your house, make sure they use these magic words before getting what they want. Overemphasize the use of these words as they nurture gratitude and humility in the heart of your grandchild.

Manner #2: Be polite when eating a meal in a restaurant or someone's home.

You can practice at home by pretending you are at a restaurant or a guest in someone's home. Explain where the utensils go, teaching your grandchild how to hold and use them correctly. This may take a lot of practice, which is just fine. Place the napkin on your lap. Do not throw food. Keep your mouth closed when chewing. Compliment the chef or thank the server. No devices allowed at the table.

Manner #3: Don't interrupt.

Using technology teaches kids that they can get what they want instantly. They are not used to waiting and can interrupt you loudly and frequently with their questions. Teach your grandchild to ask, "Is this a good time?" or to say "Excuse me" before barging in. You can also establish a hand signal, such as a child coming up to you and squeezing your hand while waiting.

A WORD ABOUT SOCIAL MEDIA

Kids and teens are getting less practice with common courtesies in real life because they are communicating via the computer, phone, video console, or tablet instead. They don't see someone's hurt expression when they text something mean or anonymously post rude comments on social media. Researchers from Johns Hopkins University found that the rate of adolescents reporting a recent bout of clinical depression grew by 37 percent between 2005 and 2014. Researchers aren't sure what's driving the rise, but they speculate that greater exposure to known depression risk factors such as problematic cellphone use, including cyberbullying, may play a role.[1]

The grandchildren you're caring for may be too young for social media. It's important for you to understand that social media is not a harmless phase that all teens must go through like a rite of passage. Although it can have a positive impact on your grandchildren, it is more likely to cause them to act in an antisocial way during their visits with you. It's okay to insist that your older grandchildren show you the common courtesy of putting away their phone during their visits. They may strongly object to this limit at first, but in the long run, your home will become a welcome break from the noisy world of social media.

In an article for the *Washington Post*, a thirteen-year-old eighth grader named Katherine said this about getting a phone and using social media:

"I don't feel like a child anymore," Katherine says.

"I'm not doing anything childish. At the end of sixth grade"—*when all her friends got phones and downloaded Snapchat, Instagram and Twitter*—*"I just stopped doing everything I normally did. Playing games at recess, playing with toys, all of it, done."*[2]

Social media is especially engaging for your granddaughters. Fifty-four percent of teens agree that using social media often distracts them from people they're with in person, and 42 percent agree that using social media takes away from time they could be spending with people face-to-face.[3]

Social media is especially engaging for your granddaughters.

As a grandparent, you can help your grandchildren silence their social media and gaming screens, so they can be more present with the people in the room. This courtesy won't just make your grandchild a pleasant dinner guest. It will give your grandchild relational skills that will make a tremendous, positive difference in his or her future family.

Positive Screen Time

What technology is actually helpful to use in my grandchild's development?

Y ou can feel like a bad grandparent if you *aren't* using technology to teach your little one. But the correlation between technology use and positive brain development is rooted more in marketing than science. All you have to do is spend one day with a child raised on a tablet compared to a child raised on books, and you'll be convinced screen time doesn't automatically produce smarter or wiser kids.

Studies have found watching educational programs such as *Sesame Street* actually has a negative, not positive, effect on language development for children younger than two years old. While you might think a TV show or app is doing a great job teaching your baby the ABCs, media use has not been proven to promote language skills in this young group. Children under two years old process information differently than older children because they are at an earlier stage of cognitive development. Young children learn language best when it's presented by a live person, not a screen.[1]

When a screen is on, that usually means conversation is at a minimum, so your grandchild loses out on listening and learning language from you. The American Academy of Pediatrics (AAP) recommends that children younger than eighteen months should avoid use of screen media except for video chatting. I (Arlene) walked in early to a women's event and noticed a woman sitting on the steps, chatting with great animation to her phone. It turns out it was her weekly call with her preschool granddaughter. That was a positive use of screen time.

For children ages two to five years, the AAP recommends limiting screen use to one hour per day of high-quality programs. Parents or grandparents should co-view with children to help them understand what they are seeing and apply it to the world around them.[2]

CHOOSE CAREFULLY

As your grandchildren get older and they are able to watch screen media, you can use these guidelines to decide whether the content is appropriate:

What factual data is my grandchild learning from this program?

If there is factual data, is it correct? You want your grandchild's mind to be filled with truth. If the program communicates a distorted vision of reality instead of how life works in the real world, you don't want your grandchild watching. You want your grandchild to be exposed to things that are real and not a distortion of reality.

What kind of character traits is this program seeking to build in my grandchild?

Is the main character someone I want my grandchild to copy? If the humor comes from cutting others down, being rude, or showing disrespect to authority, that's a red light. Positive programs will teach your child to care for others, work hard, resolve conflict, or overcome obstacles.

How does this program treat family members?

Television sitcoms often degrade men and fathers by making them lazy, fat, or stupid. What messages is your grandchild hearing about men, women, marriage, and parents? How is the family represented?

Is this program consistent with your family's values?

A child is encountering all sorts of expressions of values during his or her early years. You can't control what your child sees outside the home at school or other places, but you can control what they are exposed to during screen time at your home. What is viewed on screens should be in keeping with your family values, or it should be off limits.

After watching a TV program or movie together,

you can talk about it to enhance the experience even more. Ask questions like:

What did you learn from the program?

How do you think the main character felt when there was a problem?

What would you have done?

Having meaningful conversations is a positive way to use screens. You can use negative examples to learn lessons about what we don't want to do. For example, Cruella de Vil from *101 Dalmatians* is a black-and-white way to illustrate the commandment, "Do not steal."

CREATING VERSUS CONSUMING

If your grandchild uses screen time to learn a skill or create a product, that can have merit and value. Your grandchild might look up videos under your supervision to learn how to braid hair, cook a meal, hammer a nail, repair a flat bike tire, or learn how to play the guitar. These would be positive uses of screen media.

Encourage your grandchild to learn a skill through videos such as photography, editing, mechanics, engineering, drawing, or music. Think of screen time as either being digital vegetables or digital junk food. A little digital junk food (videos purely for entertainment) is okay, but a diet made only of junk food is not okay. Digital vegetables are online courses, tutorials, content that informs and inspires while entertaining at the same time—such as a well-done nature show. Discourage your grandchild from passively watching videos purely for amusement. Many kids will watch videos of kids skateboarding instead of grabbing a skateboard (and helmet) and riding themselves. It's unhealthy for children to *watch* life instead of *living* life.

You might wonder if it is a positive use of screen time to offer video games or social media time as a reward for completed homework or other tasks. It certainly works to offer such incentives, but we would caution against this. Melanie Hempe, RN (Ret.) and executive director of Families Managing Media, says, "Rewards should be something we value, not addictive things kids crave. Will gaming help your grandchild develop grit and a hard work ethic?" Melanie suggests using other incentives, such as time playing a game or an outing for frozen yogurt.[3]

There is so much in life that's missed when you are glued to a screen. Children must learn how to process emotions and get along with others. Those life lessons are learned best without screen media, so one of the most positive things you can do is minimize your grandchild's devices when you are together. As long as your grandchildren are coming to visit (or you are going to their house), it's not too late to turn things

It's unhealthy for children to *watch* life instead of *living* life.

around. You can decide what's a healthy use of screen time during your visits. Give it time, and your grandchildren will thrive within the boundaries you set.

Conversation Counts

How can I get my grandkids to talk to me and not just text me?

The home used to be filled by loud voices, siblings yelling across the room at one another, and kids talking on the phone with their friends. Now, instead of live voices, we hear Alexa (as in Amazon Alexa), television in the background, and the tap-tap-tap of texting. One of the pitfalls of technology has been the rapid decline of conversation. Kids and teens don't talk as much; they are learning to text and wear earbuds instead. Yet conversation has the power to cure many modern ailments such as loneliness and anxiety. As a grandparent, you have a special voice and place in the life of your granddaughter or grandson.

MAKE MOMENTS FOR CONVERSATION

One grandma writes, "My kids were brought up in the country. Our land was their playground. We brought in produce from our garden and canned a lot of fruits and vegetables. We spent plenty of time together inside and outside. Country life was the best!" During those unplugged times together, there was plenty of time for unforced, unhurried conversation.

When kids have experience talking with people, they learn to recognize the meanings of vocal inflection, body language, and facial expressions. These nuances cannot be taught by apps, video games, or robots. Children need to learn what human emotions and expressions mean through conversation.

Become a detective and play to the interests of your grandchildren. For instance, if you have a grandchild who is interested in learning how to cook, you can give them cooking lessons. If you can't cook, you can start with boiling water and end there! But if you can cook, teach your grandchild several recipes, or simple cooking practices like fixing scrambled eggs or baking a potato, over time. This will ensure your grandchild won't starve in college, and he or she will have lots of practice with making small talk in the kitchen. That will be a useful future skill in the work break room, with roommates, or with a spouse someday.

Maybe your grandchild is into music and plays the guitar. You can call and say, "Please bring your guitar over the next time you visit. I really want to hear you play!" Let your grandchildren practice and play for you. Become interested in what they are interested in. You will be able to find points for conversation from there.

Let's say your grandchild's only interest seems to be video games. Make it your goal to cultivate three other interests in your grandchild's life during your visits together. It could be anything, such as biking, baseball, knitting, woodworking, science, mechanics, fishing, dancing, creative writing, gardening, or painting. You just might be the perfect person to introduce a hobby or skill to your grandchild. Maybe your grandchild has never been to an art museum or a college basketball game. You can expose them to different activities that are available in your community. Doing an activity together is especially helpful for boys to get them talking.

Twenty Questions for Your Grandchild

What's your favorite flavor of ice cream?

(Girls) If you could be any princess for a day, who would you be and why?

(Boys) If you could be any action hero for a day, who would you be and why?

Who has been your favorite schoolteacher so far? What made him or her special?

Which gifts from last Christmas or your birthday do you still play with?

What has been your favorite family vacation?

What's a sport you would like to try?

What has been the high point of your day so far? The low point?

Think of the last time you laughed really hard. What was so funny?

When you are twenty-five years old, what kind of job do you want to have?

If you won $100, what would you do with it?

What is one thing you like about your sibling(s)?

Besides someone in your family, who is someone who is always kind to you?

What's something that really bugs you?

Do you remember the last time you got in trouble? What did you do?

What's your favorite toy?

If you could meet a person from the Bible, who would you meet?

What three vegetables do you wish did not exist?

If you could shop for free in one store for ten minutes, what shop would you pick?

What is something you have done this week to help someone?

Things to Do with Grandkids

Read aloud together.

Bake and decorate cakes.

Do arts and crafts.

Explore local museums, historic houses, nature preserves.

Attend plays and concerts.

Work on service projects like wrapping gifts for the homeless.

Look at old family photo albums and learn some family history.

Decoding Text Abbreviations

You probably already know (and maybe use!)
some of these. This is a list of some of the
most popular text abbreviations—and their
translations (this list will definitely be dated
quickly, but you get the gist). BTW (by the
way), we've given this list a "G" rating . . .
Some of these abbreviations are more (or less)
appropriate than others, but we've included the
gamut with some words amended/left out so
you can be as informed as possible.

IDK—I don't know
IKR—I know right
ILY—I love you
JK—Just kidding
K—Okay
LMK—Let me know
LOL—Laugh out loud
NVM—Never mind

OFC—Of course
OMG—Oh my gosh! Oh my goodness!
PIR—People in room (watching)
POS—Person over shoulder (watching)
ROFL—Rolling on floor laughing
SMH—Shaking my head
STFU—Shut the [blank] up
TMI—Too much information
TMRW—Tomorrow
TTYL—Talk to you later
TY—Thank you
VM—Voicemail
UR—Your, you are
W8—Wait
YOLO—You only live once
YW—You're welcome

CALLING + TEXTING

My (Arlene's) mom is a ninja at using emojis. My children don't have phones yet, but my mom will occasionally send me messages for them with rows and rows of emojis to show her love. This always makes my kids smile. Texting is a fine way to connect with your grandkids. You can text when it's convenient, and your grandkids can do the same. But don't settle for only texting. Insist on having conversations whether it's in person with your local grandkids or over the phone with your out-of-town grands. It's important to hear each other's tone of voice and connect on a much deeper level than short phrases over a text message. When you're together, set an example with your texting. If you need to respond to a text, do it briefly, explain what you're doing to your grandchild, and then put the phone down. Think of it like a hot potato.

With the grandkids who live out of your area, you almost have to set a time to talk or it won't get done. I (Gary) have found that Sunday afternoon is a good time to talk because the kids aren't in school. My granddaughter in college texts my wife and me a couple times a week and calls every Sunday afternoon. It is a habit she started in high school. The conversations usually last from fifteen to thirty minutes. It's also a habit you can initiate by calling your grandkids once a week or twice a month.

Maybe you've tried to call but you struggle over what to chat about. Your grandchild isn't very talkative. Teenagers typically aren't going to start chattering eagerly about what is going on in their lives. Also take into account different personality types; some are born yakking away, and others are quiet.

You have a lot of wisdom to pass along to your grandchild, but sometimes they need a little nudge to ask you for some.

Learn how to ask questions and listen. When you ask your grandchild direct, friendly questions about them and their lives, they will usually open up. Asking questions communicates that you are interested in their lives. They won't talk about the gymnastics event unless you ask questions. "Did lots of people compete? What were your events? Who were the judges?" Now your grandchild will talk, but they don't think of telling you unless you ask. It's our responsibility to find out what our grandkids are doing.

Another way you can encourage conversation is by saying something like, "If you could ask me any question in the world, what would you ask? You can ask me a theoretical question or a question about my childhood." You have a lot of wisdom to pass along to your grandchild, but sometimes they need a little nudge to ask you for some. During every visit, you could have a "Just ask grandma" or "Just ask grandpa" opportunity. If you give them repeated chances to ask questions, your answers will probably lead them to ask more questions, and you'll get the chance to share something that is going to be very helpful to them in the future. There's plenty to talk about, so get started today with your grandchild.

For Generations to Come

We, Arlene and Gary, are both followers of Christ. We have raised our families with this foundation and we are grateful for the influence of our own faithful parents. I (Gary) have greatly enjoyed the privilege, with Karolyn, of "grandparenting" our two grown grandkids. So we want to leave you with some thoughts about sharing the love of God with your family.

When my (Arlene's) son Ethan was little, he couldn't say "grandpa," but he could say "baba." It has been Baba ever since. My dad says this about holding Ethan, his first grandchild, for the first time: "His eyes locked on to mine. Immediately I could tell he was very special and very smart." No doubt your grandchildren were also very special and very smart—right from the start! No matter how old they are, you can continue to look into their eyes in order to communicate your love and God's love.

There are a number of ways you can have a spiritual impact on your grandchild that will last forever. One way is to ask questions about spiritual things. If they go to church, you can ask, "What did your pastor preach about on Sunday? What did you learn in Sunday school?" I (Gary) have been amazed at how they answer that question. They often heard more than I dreamed they would be able to at their ages. If they share some of their church experiences, you can respond to what they share with your own personal stories of faith.

Encourage your grandchildren to be involved in the different programs the church offers. If your grandchild needs a ride, become the driver. Maybe you attend a different church than your grandchildren and your church has midweek or camp activities for kids that their church doesn't. Invite your grandchildren to attend as long as it doesn't interrupt their normal Sunday routine with their parents. Summer Christian camp is a powerful time for a teenager to make decisions about God that can change the trajectory of their lives. When a teen is away from home, hearing other people speak at their level, they can make significant positive decisions. If your grandchild wants to go to camp but can't afford it, you may want to pay for him and a friend to go if you have the funds.

Maybe your adult children don't go to church anymore. You can gently offer to bring the grandkids to church; your adult child may say yes to have some time away from the kids. Perhaps you can relate to one grandmother named Mary, who is heartbroken that her adult son forbids her to talk about Jesus to the grandchildren. But Mary prays for her grandkids constantly and occasionally takes them to church and reads them a Bible story. Your prayers cannot be stopped. You can pray to give thanks for meals. When your grandchildren hear you pray, they get a glimpse into who you are.

William and Nancie Carmichael, authors of *Lord, Bless My Child*, have tailor-made a "Grandkid Camp" for many years with such themes as:

Olympics—Running the race (1 Cor. 9:24–27)
Star Wars—When I consider the heavens (Ps. 8)
Power of Creativity—Creation in Genesis
Using Your Talent for God—Parable of the talents (Matt. 25:14–30)

Camp is ultimately about building a relationship with your grandchildren and between the cousins and siblings. The hard work is totally worth it, says Nancie: "My husband, Bill, and I were so honored and humbled two summers ago at one of our camps when all the family gathered to baptize five of our grands in a lake near here. We rented two big pontoons for the day, and all the parents and kids were there. As they each gave their statements of faith, I thought, 'Okay God, You can take me home now. Mission accomplished!'"

THE BEST INVESTMENT

When my (Gary's) grandson, Elliott, was fourteen, I asked him, "If you could go anywhere in the world, where would you go?" To my surprise he replied,

"Papa, I would like to see the Brazilian rain forest." That blew my mind! I wasn't expecting that as an answer. He had read about the rain forest and thought it was fascinating. One month later, I received an email from my Brazilian publisher. Believe it or not, it read, "We're releasing one of your books and we would like you to come down and do a speaking tour." Can you guess how I replied? "Sure, I will come if I can bring my grandson and after the tour, we would like to have two days in the rain forest."

You can imagine the trip Elliott and I had through the rain forest with wild monkeys and alligators! Neither one of us will ever forget that. However, it certainly doesn't require an exotic environment to connect with your grandkids. The point is, you make memories together. You don't want your grandchild only to recall playing video games and watching television at your house. What favorite memories would you like your grandchildren to recall about you?

Close your eyes, taking a moment to picture it As you make these moments a reality, you will be investing in the generations that follow you. Time is a precious gift. Don't allow it to be wasted with distracting devices.

The Bible tells of a man named Abram who lived in ancient times. When he was very old, God appeared to him to change his name to Abraham and make a covenant—agreement—with him. God said, "I will establish my covenant as an everlasting covenant between me and you and your descendants after you for the generations to come, to be your God and the God of your descendants after you" (Gen. 17:7). Cry out to God on behalf of your grandchildren so that they will follow the Lord. Your example and expressions of faith play very important roles in shaping your grandchild's future. Your investment in your young grandchildren today will turn into a grand friendship and fellowship tomorrow as they become adults.

Don't allow devices to upstage your impact. *You* are the star of your grandchild's visit, not the shiny objects found in your home. And that relationship is a precious possession.

Notes

Introduction: We're Not in Kansas Anymore

1. Paula Span, "Becoming a Digital Grandparent," *New York Times*, June 5, 2019, https://www.nytimes.com/2019/06/05/well/family/kids-screen-time-grandparents.html.

Chapter 2: Video Game Wars

1. Entertainment Software Association, "2019 Essential Facts About the Computer and Video Game Industry," Entertainment Software Association, accessed June 3, 2019, https://www.theesa.com/esa-research/2019-essential-facts-about-the-computer-and-video-game-industry/.

2. Net Addiction, "The Center for Internet Addiction . . . Your Source since 1995," accessed January 2, 2020, http://netaddiction.com/kimberly-young/.

3. Tao Ran, quoted in Adam Alter, *Irresistible: The Rise of Addictive Technology and the Business of Keeping Us Hooked* (New York: Penguin Press, 2017), 252–53.

4. Entertainment Software Rating Board, accessed January 2, 2020, https://www.csrb.org/ratings-guide/.

Chapter 3: The Lure of YouTube

1. "The Disturbing YouTube Videos That Are Tricking Children," BBC, March 27, 2017, https://www.bbc.com/news/blogs-trending-39381889.

2. YouTube Kids, accessed January 2, 2020, https://www.youtube.com/kids/safer-experience/.

3. J. Clement, "Hours of Video Uploaded to YouTube Every Minute 2007-2019," Statista, August 9, 2019, https://www.statista.com/statistics/259477/hours-of-video-uploaded-to-youtube-every-minute/.

4. Josephine Bila, "YouTube's Dark Side Could Be Affecting Your Child's Mental Health," February 13 2019, CNBC, https://www.cnbc.com/2018/02/13/youtube-is-causing-stress-and-sexual-ization-in-young-children.html.

Chapter 4: Clash of the Caregivers
1. Julie Jargon, "Grandsharenting: When Grandparents Get Carried Away on Facebook," *Wall Street Journal*, November 26, 2019, https://www.wsj.com/articles/grandsharenting-when-grandparents-get-carried-away-on-facebook-11574764204.

Chapter 5: But I'm Exhausted!
1. Dimitri Christakis, "Media and Children," TEDxSeattle, December 28, 2011, video, 11:23, https://tedxseattle.com/talks/dimitri-christakis-media-and-children/.

Chapter 6: Making Common Courtesy Common Again
1. "Depression on the Rise among Teens, Especially Girls, Johns Hopkins Study Finds," Johns Hopkins University, November 16, 2016, https://hub.jhu.edu/2016/11/16/adolescent-depression-study/.

2. Quoted in Jessica Contrera, Victoria Milko, Kate Miller, and Jake Crump, "13, Right Now: This Is What It's Like to Grow Up in the Age of Likes, Lols and Longing," May 25, 2016, *Washington Post*, https://www.washingtonpost.com/sf/style/2016/05/25/13-right-now-this-is-what-its-like-to-grow-up-in-the-age-of-likes-lols-and-longing/.

3. "Social Media, Social Life: Teens Reveal Their Experiences," Common Sense Media, September 10, 2018, https://www.commonsensemedia.org/social-media-social-life-infographic.

Chapter 7: Positive Screen Time

1. Katherine Nelson, "Structure and Strategy in Learning to Talk," *Monographs of the Society for Research in Child Development* 38, no. 1/2 (February to April 1973): 1–135, http://doi.org/10.2307/1165788 and Deborah Linebarger and Dale Walker, "Infants' and Toddlers' Television Viewing and Language Outcomes," *American Behavioral Scientist* 48, no. 5 (January 2005): 624–45, https://doi.org/10.1177/0002764204271505.

2. Council on Communications and Media "Media and Young Minds," *Pediatrics* 138, no. 5 (2016), https://doi.org/10.1542/peds.2016-2591.

3. Email interview to author, December 17, 2019.

About the Authors

Gary Chapman has a passion for helping people form lasting relationships. He is the bestselling author of The 5 Love Languages® series and director of Marriage and Family Life Consultants, Inc. Gary travels the world presenting seminars, and his radio program airs on more than four hundred stations. He and his wife, Karolyn, live in North Carolina. For more information, visit his website at 5lovelanguages.com.

Arlene Pellicane is a speaker and author of several books, including *Parents Rising, 31 Days to a Happy Husband,* and *Calm, Cool, and Connected: 5 Digital Habits for a More Balanced Life.* Arlene has been a featured guest on the *Today Show, Fox & Friends, Focus on the Family,* and *FamilyLife Today,* and serves as the host of *The Happy Home* podcast. She lives in San Diego with her husband, James, and their three children. To learn more and get free family resources, visit www.ArlenePellicane.com.

HAS TECHNOLOGY TAKEN OVER YOUR HOME?

PARENTING RESOURCES

Screens and Teens applauds the good aspects of the digital age, but also alerts parents to how technology contributes to self-centered character, negative behaviors, and beliefs that inhibit spiritual growth. Dr. Kathy Koch prescribes manageable solutions regardless of your teen's technology involvement.

978-0-8024-1269-0

Calm, Cool, and Connected reveals an easy 5-step plan that will help you center your life on Jesus and love others better by decluttering your screen time. By introducing a few, easy habits into your daily routine, you can transform your relationship with technology and enjoy a life less mediated by a screen, one more full of God's presence and the presence of others.

978-0-8024-9613-3

Parents Rising shows you eight cultural trends that parents are up against today and what you can do to claim victory. This book is about growth not guilt. It's not a pep talk, or a "try harder" speech. This is real help for real problems that every parent faces.

978-0-8024-1660-5

Also available as eBooks

MOODY
Publishers

From the Word to Life

RESOURCES TO STRENGTHEN YOUR MARRIAGE

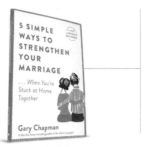

The COVID-19 pandemic has unexpectedly placed couples in unprecedented proximity. Whether sheltering in place together has been challenging or delightful for you and your spouse, let this time be an opportunity to renew your love. Learn how to do so in *5 Simple Ways to Strengthen Your Marriage... When You're Stuck at Home Together.*

978-0-8024-2332-0

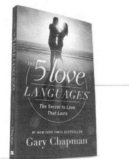

Discover the secret that has transformed millions of relationships worldwide. Whether your relationship is flourishing or failing, Dr. Gary Chapman's proven approach to showing and receiving love will help you experience deeper and richer levels of intimacy with your partner—starting today.

978-0-8024-1270-6

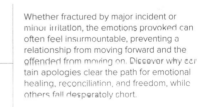

Whether fractured by major incident or minor irritation, the emotions provoked can often feel insurmountable, preventing a relationship from moving forward and the offended from moving on. Discover why certain apologies clear the path for emotional healing, reconciliation, and freedom, while others fall desperately short.

978-0-8024-0704-7

RESOURCES FOR LATER IN LIFE

Churches today often focus their resources on the early stages of discipleship. While this is important, the spiritual growth of those in the second half of life must not be neglected. Through *Becoming Sage*, reimagine the challenges of midlife as an opportunity for revitalized growth in Christ.

978-0-8024-1944-6

Empty nesting can be a disorienting time, but it can also be the best time of your life. Learn what you need to let go of and hold on to, and get practical ideas for coping and thriving in this encore season.

978-0-8024-1928-6

Nancy Kane explores the five stages of the soul's journey toward loving God. From stage one, first love, to stage five, intimate love, you will learn where you are, how to grow in love toward God and others, and how to embrace a faith that heals and fills you.

978-0-8024-1690-2

Also available as eBooks

MOODY
Publishers

From the Word to Life